How do you like our k
We would really appreciate you leaving

GW01548394

Other Picture Books:

For other fun Picture Books by Kampelstone,
simply search for:

Kampelstone Picture Books

Copyright© 2020 by Kampelstone. All rights reserved.
This book or any portion thereof may not be reproduced or used in any manner whatsoever
without the express written permission of the publisher.

Facts about Vienna

- Vienna is the largest city and the capital of Austria with 1.9 million people.

- The earliest known inhabitants in the area were Celts who settled there on the banks of the Danube in 500 BCE.

- The name Vienna is thought to come from the word vedunia which is an old German word meaning 'forest stream'. Others believe the name comes from the Celitic name Vindobona, the name the city had more than two thousand years ago. Vindobona means 'fair village' in Celtic language.

- In German, Vienna is 'Wien'(pronounced 'veen') which is today seen in English in the word wiener, the sausage used in American hot dogs.

- Vienna technically sits in two different climate zones. It's located right at the border of the moderate middle European transitional climate and the drier Pannonian zone.

- The German name for Vienna is Wien. So yes, that means Austria's most famous dish, the wiener schnitzel, translates to Viennese schnitzel. The proper serving of the dish is breaded veal with a side of parsley potatoes or a potato cucumber salad.

- The Lipizzaner stallions used in Vienna's Spanische Hofreitschule (Spanish Riding School) have kept the tradition of classical dressage alive for about 450 years.

- The famed Vienna Boys Choir has been around since 1498. Wolfgang Amadeus Mozart worked with the choir and Franz Schubert was once a member. The organization has about 100 singers between the ages of nine and fourteen who give more than 300 performances a year.

- The Vienna Giant Wheel, or Wiener Riesenrad, was built in 1897 to honor the Golden Jubilee of Emperor Franz Josef I. In 1944, it was burned down but then rebuilt the next year, and put back in rotation in 1947.

- For two years in a row, Vienna has been named the most livable city in the world.

- Every year, during the Viennese Ball Season, which runs from New Year's Eve to Shrove Tuesday more than 450 balls take place

- In Vienna, there are more than 300 vintners with about 1700 acres (7 square kilometers) of vineyards. It's the only capital city in the world with this quantity of wine production within its city limits.

- Vienna is the origin of what we now know as French croissants. Based on the Austrian kipferl (which means crescent). These pastries were designed and baked to commemorate Austria's victory over the Ottoman Turks in 1683. The shape of the kipferl is based on the crescents that were on the Ottoman soldiers' uniforms.

- Also, as a result of the defeat of the Ottomans, when the Turks fled the city, they left behind a tremendous quantity of coffee beans. Viennese Kaffeehaus culture stems from this event and has become integral to Viennese social and intellectual life.

- Just like Berlin, Vienna was divided up by the Allies at the end of World War II. The US, France, UK and the Soviet Union each took control of a part of the city until 1955 when the Austrian StateTreaty was signed.

- The Sacher Torte, Vienna's famous chocolate cake with apricot filling was invented in 1832 when Austria's Prince Metternich ordered his chef to create a new dessert for a state dinner he was hosting. It turned out that the main chef was ill that day so the creation of the new dessert fell to a 16-year-old apprentice cook named Franz Sacher.

Printed in Great Britain
by Amazon

56935151R00037